T0195934

COMPARATIVE PRACTICAL GUIDE TO SPANISH AND PORTUGUESE

A Guide to the Major Pitfalls
between the Two Languages

RUBEM LIMA

BALBOA.PRESS
A DIVISION OF HAY HOUSE

Balboa Press books may be ordered through booksellers or by contacting:

Balboa Press
A Division of Hay House
1663 Liberty Drive
Bloomington, IN 47403
www.balboapress.com
1 (877) 407-4847

Because of the dynamic nature of the Internet, any web addresses or
links contained in this book may have changed since publication and
may no longer be valid. The views expressed in this work are solely those
of the author and do not necessarily reflect the views of the publisher,
and the publisher hereby disclaims any responsibility for them.

The author of this book does not dispense medical advice or prescribe the use
of any technique as a form of treatment for physical, emotional, or medical
problems without the advice of a physician, either directly or indirectly. The
intent of the author is only to offer information of a general nature to help
you in your quest for emotional and spiritual well-being. In the event you use
any of the information in this book for yourself, which is your constitutional
right, the author and the publisher assume no responsibility for your actions.

Any people depicted in stock imagery provided by Getty Images are
models, and such images are being used for illustrative purposes only.
Certain stock imagery © Getty Images.

Print information available on the last page.

ISBN: 978-1-9822-4115-5 (sc)
ISBN: 978-1-9822-4116-2 (e)

Library of Congress Control Number: 2020900452

Balboa Press rev. date: 01/15/2020

CONTENTS

INTRODUCTION

The purpose of this book is to help speakers (native or not) of Portuguese learn Spanish and vice-versa. After many years of teaching both languages, of observing interaction between speakers of the two languages, and with the reading experience obtained in studying the literature of both languages, I have realized that their closeness is actually a formidable barrier when speakers of one try to learn the other beyond passive survival language. This problem is made clear by the fact that I have rarely met a speaker of one who spoke the other without serious flaws in semantics and pronunciation. By observing conversational interaction and intellectual discussion between the two groups of speakers, I have come to note serious misunderstandings between them because they tend to assume their cognate words or similar constructions mean the same thing.

It should be noted that mixing two different languages can be cute for about ten minutes, especially if you are a tourist just trying to get around or get the merchandise and the services you need, but can be irritating and intolerable if you are trying to establish any sort of deeper and more meaningful communication.

Also, the fact that the two languages are geographical neighbors seems to create misconceptions and stereotypes of all types in native speakers of both languages and in foreigners who learn them. Native speakers of one go around claiming to speak the other although they may never have studied or even heard the other very often. This is made worse by the fact that Americans assume that everyone speaks Spanish south of the border. This is nearly as absurd as assuming that English speakers should understand Dutch because it is a sister language.

These problems are further expanded by the unfortunate assumption by members of one group that the other language is their language "when poorly spoken" or that Portuguese "came from Spanish," ideas quickly dismissed by even a cursory reading of the history of the two languages. The point is that anyone who seriously wants to learn the other language well, beyond the level of emergency communication, realizes that the similarities are misleading, especially at a more advanced level. This confusion exists in studying any related languages: speakers of Russian have trouble learning to speak Polish well, German speakers have trouble learning Dutch, and so on.

It is hoped that this manual will be a useful

guide in staying away from the pitfalls. Experience in dealing with these two languages has shown me that the best attitude is to accept these languages as totally separate, not make any assumptions, and be thankful when similarities do appear and help the learning process.

This manual can, of course, be used by native speakers of English or of any other language who have knowledge of one language and are now trying to learn the other. They may profit from the fact that since neither Portuguese nor Spanish is their native language, they approach learning with less of a bias.

I would like to remind readers, in addition, that most languages are not mixtures of other languages, but branches or offshoots of a mother-language. Very few languages, such as English or Japanese, are considered "mixtures."

A student once asked me for tips on how to preserve his Spanish while living in Brazil and on how to keep the two languages separate. Here is my answer:

1-If at all possible, refuse to and refrain from speaking the two languages at the same time.

2-Keep them in two separate compartments in your head (you may even think of yourself as having two separate personalities (one in each language).

3-Always check on the meaning of similar-sounding

or similar-looking words. They may be complete or partial false cognates.

4-Absolutely avoid the temptation of allowing yourself to use one language to supply vocabulary you don't have in the other.

Some students have also observed that it seems easier for speakers of Portuguese to "guess at" or fake Spanish speaking and understanding than the other way around. I have to agree with that observation. This situation can be explained by many technical facts:

Firstly, Portuguese not only has more than twice as many vowels as Spanish, but has the most nasal vowels of any language on the planet. It would be very difficult for a speaker of a language with no nasal vowels to make sense of nasals in a language with many of them.

Secondly, Portuguese has a complex set of morphophonemic changes which makes sound variations in both vowels and consonants almost unpredictable and incomprehensible.

Thirdly, Portuguese has more complications in its tenses. Since it also has a very useful and far-reaching future subjunctive, it creates a lot of forms that Spanish speakers cannot guess at in a lot of situations. The use of personalized infinitive forms again create situations that are at least baffling to Spanish speakers.

SECTION 2

PHONOLOGY

2.1. Portuguese (Pg for short) has a total of 12 vowel phonemes, of which 5 are nasal. Spanish (Sp for short) has 5 oral vowels. The schwa /ə/ has a prominent place in European Pg.

2.2. It follows from the above that the 26 letters of the Pg alphabet cannot produce a good "fit" for the sounds of the language. Thus, the letter O can stand for both /o/ and /ɔ/, the letter E for both /e/ and /ɛ/. The tilde /ã/ and /õ/ can only be written over the vowels a and o, so that nasal /ɛ/, /i/, and /u/ are represented mostly be being followed by m or n.

2.3. Pg phonemes have a wide range of allophones.

2.4. There are innumerable morphophonemic changes in Pg, so that the same speaker may produce the same phoneme with markedly different qualities and consonants may be voiced or unvoiced, depending on the following consonant. Thus, 'feliz" is pronounced /feli'ʃ/ if alone, but /feli'ʒ/ in "Feliz Natal"

2.5. Pg intonation patterns are akin to that of English, not staccato, like those of Sp.

2.6. Pg phonemes are characteristically lenis,

i.e., require relatively little energy on the part of the speech organs.

2.7. Trilled r's are today rare in Pg and only a few dialects have it, where it may be in the process of disappearing and being substituted by a guttural and/or velar sound. In Brazilian Pg initial r's are glottal, i.e./h/, slightly velarized, and final r's are velar, i.e. /x/, or silent. Some uvular qualities are possible, making it a /χ/, voiceless uvular fricative.

2.8. Most Pg speakers have much difficulty producing dental slit fricatives, such as /θ/ or /ð/.

2.9. Many Pg vowels contain glides, particularly when stressed, so that one does not get the impression of pure vowels. Thus, the spelling -em stands for a nasal /ɛỹ/ (with a tilde on both vowels to indicate nasalization).

2.10. Unvoiced back vowels and regressive assimilation are distinctive features of Pg, so the word "pouco" may sound like /pokw/, where /w/ is an almost imperceptible /u/. Regressive assimilation is where the second consonant affects the first, as in " Feliz Natal"/felij nataw/(Merry Chistmas).

2.11. Note that the distinction between open and closed vowels creates contrasting words in Pg vocabulary. Thus, the only difference between" pode" (he can) and "pôde" (he could) is the constrast between the open and the closed vowel. Another example is "avô" vs."avó"(grandfather vs. grandmother).

2.12. Pg does not favor rising diphthongs, like Spanish does; Sp does not favor falling diphthongs: this fact should keep student from confusing Pg with Sp forms or from mispronouncing Pg forms that look like rising diphthongs. Thus, the 'ia" in Spanish "piadoso" is a rising diphthong, but the "ie" in Pg "piedoso" is not: the "ie" should be pronounced as two separate syllables: /pi-e-dó-zu/.

Remember that Pg has no weak vowels, so that I and u can be stressed, just like a and e.

Typically Pg has an open vowel where Sp has a split vowel: Pg pode, Sp puede. Pg cêrro, Sp cierro.

2.13. Pg intonation does not have the staccato quality of Spanish, but is more "flat" and lenis, giving almost a feeling of sleepiness. This exacerbates the differences in pronunciation.

Phonemic Comparison of Spanish and Portuguese Consonants and Vowels

Consonants		Bilabial	Labiodental	Dental	Alveolar	Alveopalatal	Velar	Glottal
Stops	vl	p			t		k	
imple	vd	[b]			[d]		[g]	
Affric.	vl					č		
	vd					[dʒ]		
Fricativ.	vl		f	θ			x	[h]
Slit	vd	(β)	[v]	(ð)			(ɣ)	
Grooved	vl				s	[š]		
	vd				[z]	[ź]		
Res.Lat.	vl				l	ʎ		

Nasal vd	m			n	ñ		
Median vd	w				y		
Flaps vd				r			
Trills vd				(ɾ)			

Vowels	Front Unrounded	Front Nasal	Central Unrounded	Central Nasal	Back Rounded	Back Nasal
High	i	[ĩ]			u	[ũ]
Higher mid	e	[ẽ]			o	
Lower mid	[ɛ]				[ɔ]	[ɔ̃]
Low			a [ə]	[ã]		

Notes on the above tables:

1-Free symbols indicate phonemes common to both languages.

2-Phonemes in parentheses () exist only as such in Sp.

3-Phonemes in brackets {} exist only as such in Pg.

4-The existence of a phoneme in in both languages does not necessarily imply that it is articulated the same or that its allophones are the same in both languages.

5-The phoneme /h/ in Portuguese has a much disputed classification and can be found in velar, glottal, or uvular position. Note that most of the time this spelled as initial "r" and shows how little parallelism there is between Sp and Pg spelling. See section on Spelling.

6-The European version of the unstressed Brazilian /a/ is higher in all positions, i.e., it is a schwa /ə/.

7-Features of Pg morphophonemics, such as palatalized consonants, backed vowels, unvoiced bowels, and y-glides on vowels should not be disregarded.

Palatalized consonants means that d and t followed by e or I are pronounced /ʤ/. Backed vowels means that final /e/ is always changed to /i/ and final /o/ is always changed to /u/, so that no Pg words end in the sounds /e/ or /o/. Words borrowed from French and other languages are exceptions, of course.

If you ask native speakers, they might deny this and give you a false stage pronunciation.

8-The phonemic classification given here is the one accepted in most textbooks of the respective languages, but is also based on my own experience and research of the Portuguese language in Lisbon and in many regions of Brazil. The culturally predominant dialect of Rio de Janeiro and the media is taken as the standard. Some variations may exist in some areas of Brazil, but they would not be considered standard.

9. Final –l is pronounced as /w/, as in Polish, so Brasil is pronounced /braziw/.

COMPARISON OF STRESSED SYLLABLES

This is a list of cognates with the same meaning, but where the stress is confusingly different from what the speaker of the other language might expect. The Italian cognates, where existing, have been added to the list. It is, of course, assumed that the reader is familiar with the basic written accent and stress rules of the respective language (Similar spelling most often does NOT indicate similar stress since Pg has no weak vowels and since the stress rules are not the same). Genders may not coincide in the three languages. Where a suitable cognate is not available, the column is left blank. Only nouns have been pulled for comparison. Some cognates may show forms with additional confusing characteristics, such as unexpected suffixes. Many cognate verbs will have stress on a different syllable than the other language because of the peculiar stress patterns of each language.

Note that Pg has no injunction against using the feminine definite article before feminine words starting with stressed "a:" Compare Pg *a alma* with Sp *el alma*.

SPANISH	PORTUGUESE	ITALIAN
academia	academia	academia
acróbata	acrobata	acrobata
albumina	albumina	albumina
alcohol	álcool	alcool
alguien	alguém	qualcuno
alquimia	alquimia	alchimia
anatema	anathema	anathema
anecdota	anedota	aneddoto
anemia	anemia	anemia
anestesia	anestesia	anestesia
ariete	ariete	ariete
aristocracia	aristocracia	aristocrazia
aristócrata	aristocrata	aristocratico
arnica	arnica	arnica
asfixia	asfixia	asfissia
astenia	astenia	astenia
atmósfera	atmosfera	atmosfera
atrofia	atrofia	atrofia
azoe	azoe	azoe
burocracia	burocracia	burocrazia
burócrata	burocrata	burocrate
bigamia	bigamia	bigamia
cabala	cabala	cabala

canguro	cangurú	canguro
canibal	canibal	cannibale
cartílago	cartilagem	cartilagine
cenit	zenite	zenite
cerebro	cérebro	cerebro
chofer	chofer	----------
difteria	difteria	difterite
diócesis	diocese	diocesi
Dios	Deus	Dio
diplomacia	diplomacia	diplomazia
dispepsia	dispepsia	dispepsia
dispnea	dispnéia	dispnea
Edén	Éden	Eden
elite	elite	elite
elogio	elogio	elogio
endocrino	endócrino	endocrino
endoscopia	endoscopia	endoscopia
epidemia	epidemia	epidemia
error	êrro	errore
fobia	fobia	fobia
gaucho	gaúcho	gaucho
hemofilia	hemofilia	emofilia
hemorragia	hemorragia	emorragia
héroe	herói	eroe
hidrofobia	hidrofobia	idrofobia
hidrógeno	hidrogênio	idrogeno

hipertrofia	hipertrofia	ipertrofia
homeopata	homeopata	omeopatico
idiosincrasia	idiosincrasia	idiosincrasia
imán	imã	--------------
imbécil	imbecil	imbecille
impar	ímpar	impari
lila	lilá	lilla
límite	limite	limite
liturgia	liturgia	liturgia
magia	magia	magia
mediocre	medíocre	mediocre
metalurgia	metalurgia	metallurgia
miope	míope	miope
neuralgia	neuralgia	nevralgia
neurastenia	neurastelnia	nevrastenia
nitrógeno	nitrogênio	nitrogeno
nivel	nível	livello
ortopedia	ortopedia	ortopedia
oxígeno	oxigênio	ossigeno
pantano	pântano	pantano
pensil	pênsil	pensile
Pentecostés	Pentecostes	Pentecoste
periferia	periferia	periferia
perineo	perineo, perineu	-----------
peritoneo	peritônio, peritoneu	peritoneo

perone	perônio, peroneu	perone
piloro	piloro	piloro
plétora	pletora	pletora
plutocracia	plutocracia	plutocrazia
policia	polícia	polizia
prototipo	protótipo	prototipo
psoriasis	psoríase	soriasi
pudico	pudico	pudico
reina	rainha	regina
reptil	réptil	rettile
reverbero	revérbero	----------
ricino	rícino	ricino
siderurgia	siderurgia	siderurgia
síntoma	sintoma	sìntomo
taquicardia	taquicardia	tachicardia
textil	textil	tessile
tráquea	traquéia	trachea
vitriolo	vitriolo	vetriolo

SECTION 4

GENDERS

The following is a list of words in the two languages which are close enough in form, but in which the genders do not agree. Words in –aje(Sp) and –agem Pg have not been included because they are perfectly predictable: all Sp masculines in –aje correspond to Pg feminines in –agem, such as Sp *el garaje*, Pg *a garagem*. A few words in Pg can be episcene, i.e., can have either gender.

List one:
Masculine in Spanish, feminine in Portuguese

un aluvión	uma aluvião
un análisis	uma análise
un apocalipsis	uma apocalipse
un árbol	uma árvore
un avestruz	uma avestruz
un cartílago	uma cartilagem
um caudal	um(a)caudal (episcene)
un cobayo	uma cobaia
un color	uma cor
un crater	uma cratera

un cutis	uma cútis
un champaña	uma champanhe
un desorden	uma desordem
un dolor	uma dor
un epígrafe	uma epígrafe
un estreno	uma estréia
un fraude	uma fraude
un estante	uma estante
un insomnio	uma insonia
un orden	uma ordem
un orígen	uma origem
un orín	uma urina
un panqueque	uma panqueca
un platino	uma platina
un puente	uma ponte
un rezo	uma reza
un síncope	uma síncope
un sonrisa	um sorriso
un testimonio	uma testemunha
un torrente	uma torrente
un vals	uma valsa
un vértigo	uma vertigem

LIST 2:
Feminine in Sp, masculine in Pg

un(a) azúcar	um açucar
una aspiradora	um aspirador
una baraja	um baralho
una brea	um breu
una cárcel	um cárcel
una cima	um cimo
una computadora	um computador
una costumbre	um costume
una coz	um coz
una crema	um creme
una creciente	um crescente
una diadema	um diadema
una dote	um dote
una enseñanza	um ensino, um ensinamento
una estrategema	um estratagema
una grabadora	um gravador
una guia	um guia (book)(the profession is episcene)
una hiel	um fel
una hormona	um hormônio
una labor	um labor
una leche	um leite
una legumbre	um legume

una lumbre	um lume
una mar, un mar	um mar
una mascota	um mascote
una melaza	um melaço
una miel	um mel
una nariz	um nariz
una pampa	um pampa
una pesa (weight for exercise)	um pêso
una pesadilla	um pesadelo
una protesta	um protesto
una rama	um ramo
una risa	um riso
una samba	um samba
una sangre	um sangue
una sonrisa	um sorriso
una traza	um traço
una ubre	um úbere
una vislumbre	um vislumbre

SECTION 5

SPELLING

5.1. Pg spelling rules are controlled by the Portuguese Academy of Sciences and the Brazilian Academy of Letters and may change every now and then.

5.2. Pg spelling rules are many, complex, often inconsistent, and can only be learned by rote. Written accents are acute, grave, and circumflex. The tilde is used over a and o to show nasalization. There is also a c cedilla (ç) with the value of unvoiced /s/. Sp has simple rules for the use of the acute accent.

5.3. Note that Pg does not have a system of weak vowels (SP *i* and *u*), so that similar spelling in the two languages actually indicates different stress, in addition to the phonemic differences. Compare Pg *aristocracia* and Sp *aristocracia*

5.4 Sp spelling rules are controlled by the Royal Spanish Academy and change very little.

5.5. Pg words do not normally end in –n but must use –m, unless they were borrowed from Latin or other foreign languages. Pg cannot pronounce final –n or –m, so –am is pronounced as a nasal /aw/ and /em/ as a nasal /ey/.

SECTION 6

MORPHOLOGY

6.1. There are 6 types of plural inflection in Pg and 2 in Sp.

6.2. There are about 150 words in Pg with meaning altogether different from that of their Sp cognates.

6.3. There are about 70 Pg words with gender different from that of their Sp cognates.

6.4. There are about 70 words with stress different from that of their Sp cognates. Endings such as –cia, -crata, gia, etc, are typically stressed –cia, -crata, -gia in Pg.

6.5. About 75 Sp and Pg cognates have spellings that are utterly confusing to a Pg speaker trying to learn Sp and vice-versa. E.g. Pg *escrever* and Sp *escribir* (notice the change in conjugation).

6.6. Names of plants, animals, articles of clothing, etc. may be very different in form and may have completely different origins.

6.7. Pg has only one set of possessives. Compare Pg *o meu* with Sp *mi, el mío.*

6.8. Pg has 3 sets of endings in the preterite (one for each of the first three conjugations); Sp has 2.

6.9. The future subjunctive is an everyday tense

in Pg and is more commonly used than the future indicative, which can always be substituted by the periphrastic future or the present. The Sp future subjunctive is rarely used and is nearly defunct. The future subjunctive has to be used in Pg if the condition has to do with future time or is generic. Sp uses present subjunctive in these cases.

6.10. There is a number of differences in the use of the present subjunctive in the two languages, even beyond uses that would logically be covered by the Pg future subjunctive.

6.11. Note that Pg has a "personal infinitive" form that no other Indo-European language has: *O falarmos Português é importante* (Our speaking Portuguese is important).

6.12. There are many contractions of preposition and article (i.g., *da, num*) and demonstrative and article (e.g., *nessas, naquelas*) in Pg.

6.13. Pg has a synthetic pluperfect tense, mostly used in writing. Its forms (-ara, *-era, -ira* for each conjugation, respectively) can easily be confused with the Sp imperfect subjunctive forms in *–ara, -iera*.

6.14. The gerund has four forms in Pg, one for each conjugation (e.g., *falando, escrevendo, abrindo, pondo*). In Sp it has only two forms, one for the -ar and another for the –er and –ir conjugations (*hablando, bebiendo, abriendo*).

SECTION 7

FORMS

This is a list with close, but often confusing, forms. It should be noted that many times a difference of a single letter may put a verb in a totally different conjugation pattern than the one it belongs to in the other language.

Thus, the confusion starts with the infinitive and goes on through all conjugated forms. Also, verbs with minor irregularities in the two languages frequently show that irregularity in a different form (Compare Pg *se veste* with Sp *se viste*, Pg *repete* with Sp *repite*, Pg *prefiro* with Sp *prefiero*).

Words may also differ in gender and grammatical function. The fact a noun differs in meaning does not necessarily mean that the corresponding cognate adjectives also will.

Speakers need to pay a lot of attention to the fact that Pg tends to have far more irregular past participles than Spanish and not assume that participles are similar or the same: compare Sp pagado, Pg pago; Sp confundido, Pg confuso, etc.

In medical terminology, Pg prefers −ose and −logista, where Spanish has −osis and −ólogo.

All Parts of Speech

SPANISH	PORTUGUESE
abofetear	esbofetear
acondicionado	condicionado
afirmar (an object, e.g., a ladder)	firmar
agotar	esgotar
aguantar	aguentar
aislar	isolar
apertura	abertura
a pesar de	apesar de
apóstol	apóstolo
armonia	harmonia
arrollar	enrolar
así asá	assim assado
atontado	tonto
avaluar	avaliar
bailarín	bailarino
bajar	abaixar
batir	bater
bendecido	bendito
bloque	bloco
brujería	bruxaria
cantidad	quantidade
carbón	carbono

cascada	cascata
ceremonia	cerimônia
científico	cientista
cirugía	cirurgia
cirujano	cirurgião
combatir	combater
compás	compasso
comprender	compreender
confort	comfôrto
convertir	converter
cono	cone
coordinar	coordenar
corregir	corrigir
costarricense	costariquense
crema	crema
cumplido	cumprimento
chino	chinês
dato	dado
decir	dizer
defensa	defesa
demostración	demonstración
demostrar	demonstrar
desenmascarar	desmascarar
desilusionar	desiludir
derrumbar	derrubar
dinero	dinheiro

diplomático	diplomata
disminución	disminuição
dósis	dose
efímero	efêmero
elemental	elementar
empeorar	piorar
enfasizar	enfatisar
enganoso	enganador
entremeter	intrometer
entrenar	treinar
escribir	escrever
esquimal	esquimó
estadística	estatística
estancia	estadia
estatal	estatal (national), estadual (state)
escupir	cuspir
estiércol	estêrco
evaluación	avaliação
exiliar	exilar
experimentado	experiente
exprimir	expremer
faraón	faraó
farmacólogo	farmacologista
fondo	fundo
humear	defumar

gemir	gemer
general	geral
glucemia	glicemia
glucosa	glucose
golosina	guloseima
hamburguesa	hambúrger
hipocresía	hipocrisia
hombro	ombro
hormón, hormona	hormônio
hipertiroidismo	hipertireoidismo
impulsar	impulsionar
innecesario	desnecessário
innovación	inovação
insertar	inserir
interrumpir	interromper
invertir	investir
invertir	inverter
jeringa	seringa
lamer	lamber
lámpara	lâmpada
leer	ler
liberación	libertação
linterna	lanterna
llano	plano
marcapasos	marca-passo
mermelada	marmelada

manantial	manancial
mañana	manhã (morning)
	amanhã (tomorrow)
mariscal	marechal
mensual	mensal
metrópoli	metrópole
milagro	milagre
muelle	mole
múltiple	múltiplo
nicaragüense	nicaraguano
noruego	norueguês
noticiero	noticiário
ortopedia	ortopedia
orquesta	orquestra
pagado	pago (past participle)
pago	pagamento (noun)
palidecer	empalidecer
pérdida	pêrda
piadoso	piedoso
pino	pinho
pintoresco	pitoresco
plan	plano
plano	planta
póliza	pólice
pregunta	perguntar
prensa	imprensa

presentar	apresentar
prestar	apresentar
prieto	prêto
progresar	progredir
prójimo (person), próximo(next)	próximo
propio	próprio
prórroga	prorrogação
quiropráctico	quiróprata
receta	receita
relojero	relojoeiro
rencor	rancor
repercutar	repercutir
revisar (a person, luggage)	revistar
reseñar	revisar
recibir	receber
romería	romaria
ruta	rota
salival	salivar
salvaje	selvagem
sarampión	sarampo
si	se
simple	simples
sofocar	sufocar
soportar	suportar

sorprender	sorpreender
suplementario	suplementar
tarea	tarefa
tierno	tenro
toser	tossir
tráquea	traquéia
trastorno	transtorno
trasplante	transplante
trasto	traste
trastorno	transtorno
tráfico	tráfego(cars), tráfico(drugs)
truco	truque
vacunación	vacinação
zapatería	sapataria

SECTION 8

SYNTAX

1.Pronoun use:

1.1. Beginning sentences with unstressed personal pronouns is not sanctioned by grammar in Pg, although done informally. Compare Sp *lo veo* with Pg *vejo-o*.

1.2. Mesoclisis (pronoun in the middle) is possible in Pg both in the future and in the conditional:
Falar-lhe-ei, falar-lhe-ia.

1.3. The Pg direct or indirect object pronouns can go before or after the verb : *vejo-o. Não o vejo.*
Fala-se Português. Aqui se fala Português.

1.4. The direct object in Pg cannot be preceded by a preposition, as is the rule in Sp if the object is animate. Exceptions are stylistic and rare.

1.5. Pg speakers drop the reflexive pronouns with reflexive verbs in informal speech: *Levanto as 7*, instead of *levanto-me as 7*.

1.6. Informal Brazilian speech has a tendency to use subject pronouns for the object pronouns, although the usage us not grammatically sanctioned: *Eu vi ele* for *Eu o vi.*

2. Note the widespread use of the definite article

with possessives and proper names in Pg: *o meu carro, a Maria.*

3.In Pg the preposition *a* cannot be used with the periphrastic future: *Sp voy a almorzar, Pg vou almoçar.*

4. In Pg the preposition *a* cannot be used between the verb vir and a following infinitive: *Sp vengo a almorzar, Pg venho almoçar.*

5.Like English and very few other languages, Pg commonly uses tag answers in speech: *Falo, sim* (notice that the affirmative adverb follows the verb). The negative adverb precedes the verb and may be doubled in informal speech: *Não falo (não).*

6. Pg does not use a reflexive construction when referring to parts of the body: *lavo as mãos.*

7. To play: The Pg verb *jogar* cannot have a before the name of a game: Sp *jugar al fútbol*, Pg *jogar futebol.*

8. The use of prepositions, even if cognate, may be evidently or subtly different in two languages. Thus, Pg may only use *em* with *entrar,* never *a.*

9. A preposition must be used in Pg before the days of the week: *Sp does not use one. E.g. Pg aos domingos, Sp los domingos.*

10. The comparative of *grande* must be *maior* in Pg, but it is *más grande* in Sp.

11. Idiomatic spoken Pg uses an expletive question reinforcement (é que) 90% of the time between the interrogative word and the verb: *Onde é que está o livro?*

12. Pg frequently labels direct and indirect verbs differently. Thus, *assistir a* and *atender a* are always indirect verbs in Pg and must be prepositioned.

13. Pg does not accept the article before dates. The idiomatic usage is either no article or inserting the word *dia* before the date: *dia 11 de outubro*, Sp *el 11 de octubre.*

14. The indirect object may not be repeated in Pg, thus pg *dou-lhe o livro* vs. Sp *le doy el libro a él.*

15. Pg uses a connector with all numbers, not just between tens and digits: *Cp.Sp dos mil uno, Pg dois mil e um.*

SECTION 9

SEMANTICS

1.There are over 160 cases of close cognates with completely different meanings.

2.There are many cases where a Pg and Sp cognates may both similar and different meanings, e.g. Pg *procurar* and Sp *procurar*.

3. A cognate carrying main responsibility for a given meaning in a language may be archaic, specialized, or carry social labels in another: compare Pg *prêto* and Sp *prieto*.

4. Pg has a synthetic pluperfect tense, mostly used in writing. Its forms (-ara, *-era, -ira* for each conjugation, respectively) can easily be confused with the Sp imperfect subjunctive forms in *–ara, -iera*.

5. The compound past always has a recent and continuing connotation in Pg and cannot be used in an indefinite sense, so it differs from the present perfect in English and the perfecto in Spanish. Thus, it must always be followed by an expression of unfinished time: *Tenho trabalhado muito este ano.*

The following is a list of the "false friends" I have collected over years of teaching Sp and Pg. "False friends" refers to the fact that these words do not mean what they appear to mean to speakers of the other language. While a few of these words are uncommon, most of them are everyday words and would obviously lead to misunderstanding or offense if assumed to mean what they do not. Most differences are gross, but some can be very subtle. Some word may differ in gender or grammatical function, besides meaning. It is possible that some words may have had an identical meaning at some point in history closer to the original Latin, but started to diverge or become specialized with the passing of time as Sp and Pg became more distant from each other. Note that even words with exactly the same spelling may not necessarily be pronounced the same in both languages since their spelling rules and phoneme inventories rarely match.

SPANISH TO PORTUGUESE: Masculine nouns:

abrigo=coat, shelter	abrigo=shelter
aceite=oil, olive oil	azeite=oil (food only)
acento=stress, accent	acento=written accent or stress mark.
apellido=family name	apelido=nickname, nom de guerre
balcón=balcony	balcão=service counter
barullo=confusion	barulho=noise, trouble

billón=10 to the 11th power	bilhão=billion
bizcocho=sponge cake	biscoito=cookie
broche=brooch, staple	broche-brooch
cachorro-cub, puppy	cachorro=dog
cambalache=exchange, swap, secondhand shop	cambalache=swindle, fraud
candelero=candlestick	candeeiro=kerosene lamp
canon=canyon, gun barrel, cannon	canhão=cannon
capacho=basket	capacho=doormat
caracol=conch	caracol=snail
casco=helmet, hulk, hoof	casco=hoof, boat hull
concertar=to agree	concertar= to repair
coma=coma, comma	coma=coma
copo=bundle of cotton	copo=drinking glass
constipación=constipation	constipação=plugged nose due to cold
coquero-cocaine user or dealer	coqueiro=coconut tree
cuello=neck	colo=lap
chatear=to chat on computer	chatear=to annoy, bore
chorizo=smoked pork sausage	chouriço=blood sausage
desaguisado=offense	desaguisado=conflict

despacho=spiritual offerings

despacho=black magic offerings

despecho=spite

despeito=spite, envy

engaño=trick

engano=mistake

escaño=bench

escanho=shave (old-fashioned)

escritorio=desk

escritório=office

fogón=fireplace (-box), stove

fogão=stove

globo=globe, balloon

globo=globe

gozo=praise

gôzo=enjoyment

gremio=union, society

grêmio=sport club

hospicio=lodging

hospício=mental institution

humo=smoke

fumo=smoking (tobacco or marijuana)

influjo=influence, inflow

influx=inflow

juzgado=court of justice

julgado=defendant

jardín=garden, yard

jardim=flower garden

ladrillo=brick, tile

ladrilho=tile

lapisero=pen, pencil sharpener, pencil

lapiseira=mechanical pencil, box

liga=league, garter, alloy, rubber band

liga=league, garter, alloy

logro=attainment

lôgro=cheat, bluff

mascote=mascot, pet

mascote=mascot

menino=servant

menino=boy

millo=millet

milho=corn

mostrador=counter

mostrador=showcase

mozo=servant, waiter

môço=young man, chap

oral=edge, border

oral=oceanfront

padre=father, priest

padre=priest

palco=theater box

palco=theater stage

pantano=marsh, reservoir, trouble

pântano=marsh, bog

parahuso=jeweler's bowl

parafuso=screw

párvulo=small child

parvo=idiot

pastel=cake, pastry, meat pie (Arg.)

pastel=triangular meat pie

pastilla=pill

pastilha=lozenge

pelo=hair, fur

pêlo=fur

pimpollo=rosebud, sapling

pimpôlho=small child

pingado=penis (slang)

pingado=coffee with milk (Sp cortado)

rasgo=trait, feat

rasgo=tear

recelo=suspicion

receio=fear

regalo=gift

regalo=pleasure, delight

romance=romance

romance=romance, novel

sobrado(Chile)=haughty person

sobrado=house with 2 levels

sótano=basement

sótano=attic

suceso=happening

sucesso=success

taller=workshop	talher=table silver
telón=curtain theater	telão=advertising curtain
taza=cup	taça=wine or champagne glass, sportscup
traje=suit	traje=costume
trillón=10 to the 17th power	trilhão=trillion
trozo=piece, excerpt	troço=thingummibob, penis
truque=game of cards	truque=trick
vaso=drinking glass, vase, duct	vaso=vase, toilet bowl
zonzo=dimwit, dullard	sonso=shammer, cheater

SPANISH TO PORTUGUESE: Feminine nouns

almohada=pillow	almofada=cushion
anecdota=tale	anedota=tale
batata=sweet potato	batata=potato
batuta=stick	batuta=stick; slick or skillful person
bazofia=garbage	bazófia=vanity (personal)
biznaga=joke	bisnaga=loaf of bread, tube (toothpaste, etc)

borracha=drunk woman	borracha=rubber
borrachera=drunken spell	borracheira=tire dealer
broma=joke, jest, fun	broma (m)=stupid fellow
calzada=highway, causeway	calçada=sidewalk
cachaza=sloth, phlegm, rum	cachaça=sugar cane brandy
caneca=glazed earthen bottle	caneca=mug
capa=cloak	capa=magazine cover, raincoat
carroza=coach, parade float	carroça=(ox)cart
cara=face	cara=face(pejorative), "mug"
cola=tail, glue	cola=glue
cobra=team of mares	cobra=snake
coima=concubine, bribe	coima=fine (archaic)
comarca-region	comarca=legal district
comparsa=theater extra	comparsa (m)=accomplice
copa=goblet	copa=pantry, (championship) cup
cuadrilla=group, crew	quadrilha=group of gangsters, square dance

cueca=folk dance of Chile and Bolivia

cueca=man's underpants

descubierta-reconnoitering

descuberta=discovery

escoba=broom

escova=brush of any kind

falda=skirt

fralda=diaper

firma=firm, signature

firma=firm, notary signature

fluidez=fluency, fluidity

fluidez=fluidity

ganancia=gain, profit

ganância=greed, gluttony

garrucha=pulley

garrucha=pistol

goma-rubber, glue

goma=gum, starch, glue

granja=farm

granja=chicken farm

habitación=room, housing

habitação=housing

jerigonza=jargon

jeringonça=jalopy, trash

maca=bruise, defect

maca=stretcher (medical)

madre=mother

madre=(Catholic) sister

mariposa=butterfly

mariposa=moth

marmita=boiler

marmita=lunch pail

menina=servant girl

menina=girl

muñeca=doll

munheca=wrist

novela=novel

novela=short story, soap opera

oficina=office

oficina=garage, mechanic's shop

orquesta=musical group, orchestra

orquestra=orchestra

pipa=pipe, wine cask

pipa=kite, wine cask

prenda=security, pawn, garment, talent

prenda=talent, skill

querella=complaint

querela=quarrel, complaint

quinta=villa, draft

quinta=park, piece of land

rabanada=slice of breade

rabanada=tail lash, Christmast toast

taza=cup

taça=(sports)cup, wine or champagne glass

tela=cloth

tela=screen of any kind

tienda=store, tent

tenda=tent

toalla=towel

toalha=tablecloth, towel

tontería=stupidity.

tonteira=dizziness.

valla=fence, barricade

vala=ditch

vírgula=rod, dash

vírgula=comma

visualidad=pleasant aspect

visualidade=changing aspect

SPANISH TO PORTUGUESE: Verbs

apresar=to grasp, hasten	apressar=to hasten
acordar=to resolve	acordar=to wake up
aborrecer=to upset, bore, detest	aborrecer=to upset, bore
acarretar=to carry in a cart	acarretar=to cause to happen
apremiar=to compel, harass	premiar=to give a prize
aparar=to adorn	aparar=to support, trim
bonificar=to give a discount	bonificar=to give a bonus
borrar=to erase	borrar=to blot, smear
botar=to throw out	botar=to put
brincar=to bounce, be touchy	brincar=to play
comprovar=to prove, check	comprovar=to prove, attest
conozco=I know	conosco= with us (prep.+ pronoun)
concertar=to agree on	consertar=to fix
contester=to answer	contestar=to contest
chingar=bother, annoy, have sex (vulgar)	chingar=to call bad names
chocar=to hit (a car, etc)	chocar=to hatch, to shock, to hit (a car, etc.)

embarrazar=to make pregnant

embaraçar=to embarrass, tangle

embromar=to joke with

embromar=to delay, attempt to confuse

encomendar=to commend

encomendar=to order (a book, etc)

enderezar=to straighten

endereçar=to address

enojar=to anger, annoy

enojar=to disgust

entornar=to squint, leave ajar, upset

entornar=to spill liquids

exprimir=to exploit, wring out

exprimir=to express

fallar=to fail, pass judgement

falhar=to fail

halagar=to flatter

alagar=flood

jugar=to play (general)

jogar=to play (specific game or sport)

latir=to beat

latir=to bark (dogs)

lograr=to attain, manage

lograr=to manage, cheat

marcharse=to leave

marchar=to march

mirar=to look

mirar=to aim, target

pegar=to hit, beat up

pegar=to pick up, stick

picar=to itch, to bite(mosquito)

picar=to shred, to bite(mosquito)

procurar=to try to, intend

procurar=to try to, intend, look for

requebrar=to falter	requebrar=to swing the hips
tirar=to throw, draw, shoot	tirar=to remove, withdraw
tocar=to touch, beat	tocar=to play music, touch, sound (bell, phone)
trasladar=to move	transladar=to move a corpse

SPANISH TO PORTUGUESE: All other parts of speech

a menudo=often	amiude=quickly
anoche=last night	à noite=at night
avisado=prudent	avisado=warned
bermejo=dark red(archaic)	vermelho=red
desaforado=excessive	desaforado=insolent
distinto=clear, different	distinto=honorable, clear, different
exquisito=exquisite	exquisito=queer, weird
¡Felicidades! Congratulations!	Felicidades! Good luck!
largo=long	largo=broad, wide
medroso=dreadful, scared	medroso=afraid

parado=standing, stopped	parado=stopped, quiet
pronto=soon (adverb)	pronto=ready (adjective)
pulcro=caring	pulcro=pretty
rojo=red	roxo=purple
rubio=blond	ruivo=red-haired
sesudo=wise	sisudo=grave, serious, stocky (adverb)
todavía=still	todavia=nevertheless, however (conjunction)
tonto=stupid, foolish	tonto=dizzy, careless

VOCABULARY CHOICE

The two languages often differ in word choice for different situations, even if they have the same cognate root. E.g.: *resbalar* is used for cars sliding in Spanish, but not in Portuguese, which prefers *deslizar*. Using *resvalar* for bullets and rocks. When it comes to advanced vocabulary, choices of verbs and adjectives for the two languages can be very challenging to the speaker of one of them because there are often 2 or 3 meanings that match, but 2 or 3 meanings that do not.

BRAZILIAN VS. EUROPEAN PORTUGUESE

As happens between Britain and the US, the accent and the choice of words is not the same in Brazil as in Portugal. This is a bonus list of words that are different in meaning in the two major Portuguese speaking countries:

Brazilian Word	European Word
A	
abajur	candeeiro
abridor de garrafas	abre garrafas
açougue	talho
aluguel	aluguer, renda
armazém	empório
atadura	ligadura
B	
babador	babeiro
bala	rebuçado
banca	quiosque
bandaid	adesivo
banheiro	casa (quarto) de banho
barbante	cordel

barbeador elétrico	máquina de barbear
blazer	casaco desportivo
bonde	eléctrico
boné	touca
buate	night club
bunda (familiar)	cú

C

café da manhã	pequeno almoço
cafezinho	bica
calcinha	cueca
camisola	camisão de dormir
camping	campismo
canadense	canadiano
capa de chuva	impermeável
carbono	papel químico
cardápio	ementa
carneiro	borrego
carregador	bagageiro
carteira de motorista	carta de condução
casaco	camisola de lã
champú	champô
clipe	pinça
cobrador	revisor
comutador de mínimos	interruptor de faróis
contador	contabilista
couve	couve-lombardea

creme	crema
cruzamento	encruzilhada
cú=asshole	ôlho do cú=asshole
D	
de carona	à boleia
defumado	fumado
denim	sarja
depósito	cacifo
desodorante	desodorizante
desportivo	de desporto
distrito policial	posto policial
E	
eixo de hélice	eixo accionador
empregada	criada
endereço	direcção
entrada	bilhete
esmalte	verniz
esparadrapo	adesivo
estação ferroviária	caminho de ferro
estrada de ferro	linha férrea
F	
fazenda	quinta
feche eclair	fecho de correr
ferrovia	caminho de ferro
fósforo	lume
formula	impresso

freio	travão
frutos do mar	mariscos
G	
garçom	criado de mesa
garçonete	criada de mesa
gim	genebra
grapefruit	toranja
H	
hambúrger	hamburgo
I	
Imposto de renda	imposto profissional
ipsilom	i-grego
L	
laquê	laca
linguiça	chouriço
liquidificador	misturador
lixa de unhas	lima de cartão
M	
marrom	castanho
meias	peúgas
menú	ementa
milkshake	batido
moça	rapariga
N	
na hora	a horas
não amarrota	inrugável

nos fundos	nas traseiras
P	
paletó	casaco
parada	paragem
passagem	bilhete
pegar	apanhar
pendente	pingente
pica	picadura
pipa	papagaio
ponto final	terminus
presunto	fiambre
privada	retrete
Q	
quadril	anca
querosene	petróleo
quitanda	hortaliceiro
R	
ramal	interno
raquete	raqueta
registrar	registar
rosto	cara
S	
salgadinho	acepipe
salva-vidas	banheiro
sobrenome	apelido
soda	água de sifão

sorvete	gelado
suiças	patilhas

T

talco	pó de talco
terno	fato
térreo	rés-do-chão
toca-discos	gira-discos
traje	trajo
travesseiro	almofada
trem	comboio

V

vagão leito	carruagem cama
ventilador	ventoinha
vermelho	encarnado
vitamina (de frutas)	batido

Printed in the United States
By Bookmasters